nailed down

Also by Julian Edney

Greed: A treatise

nailed down

poems by
julian edney

iUniverse, Inc.
New York Lincoln Shanghai

nailed down

Copyright © 2006 by Julian Edney

All rights reserved. No part of this book may be used or reproduced by any means, graphic, electronic, or mechanical, including photocopying, recording, taping or by any information storage retrieval system without the written permission of the publisher except in the case of brief quotations embodied in critical articles and reviews.

iUniverse books may be ordered through booksellers or by contacting:

iUniverse
2021 Pine Lake Road, Suite 100
Lincoln, NE 68512
www.iuniverse.com
1-800-Authors (1-800-288-4677)

ISBN-13: 978-0-595-38454-9 (pbk)
ISBN-13: 978-0-595-82834-0 (ebk)
ISBN-10: 0-595-38454-4 (pbk)
ISBN-10: 0-595-82834-5 (ebk)

Printed in the United States of America

Contents

perhaps that scream was from a public bathroom 1

coarse breathing 2

calling Rothenberg's dogs 4

abject 6

expert at street drains 7

get these paintings through the fence 8

abyss 10

vacancy maps 12

possession 14

whisper 15

shift shoe 16

tango 17

the day's later light 18

Nebraska, walking 19

magnets in my boots 20

secrecy 21

sahara eye 23

a lull in the fighting 25

folded roofs 27

factory girl 29

drawing 30

storm 31

squint 32

by night 33

day of Esther's cat 34

orchard dogs 37

waiting on a chair 38

my couch wants to be water 40

night fight 41

Passiod's song 44

cello 47

lessons from a cat on waiting 49

slow rented rooms 50

a low sociopathic hotel 51

at the Linnington Café 53

I bicycled the desert 55

the groin and grain of frosted land 56

in heat 57

1930 59

tin by tin 61

Grateful acknowledgement is made to the following publications in which some of these poems have appeared:

Beloit Poetry Journal "cello"
Lullwater Review "waiting on a chair," "my couch wants to be water," "Nebraska, walking"
Seneca Review "groin and grain of frosted land"
Wisconsin Review "the day's later light"
The Pacific Review "in heat"
Echo 681 "factory girl"

perhaps that scream was from a public bathroom

some use a star, clarity placed and direction gives hope
but here wind clatters unbalanced,
the slow night turns, stars flicker out.
a scream provides direction to walk away from.

a scream is a hinge, it opens
and from that places to tread unfold corners
fleeing steps dismantled in the evening.

now this: a gunshot which reassembles its ripples
is no use because I have no idea where it came from.
these empty pockets while walking

in and out of a year. and I smile as I have no idea what's going on.
but these dirty insides of boots keep taking this week
past windows, through open lots

this year's been the biggest piece of furniture I ever carried.
-another scream, geometry of a chrome hubcap
it came from in that alley

and my subtracted running steps, tipping
diagonal across the dainty night, translucently
just right for screams, each arch iridescent.

after the darkest pause city trees collect daylight
between their tips like rat traps going off.
no stars and no direction

and morning will collect, like a filling sail. other sounds,
and then bulges a smoothed day, tight, yellow, indifferent, discordant.

coarse breathing

the sun walks backwards towards evening
a kind of theft

and outside my apartment window
that leafy tree is a crowd of flickering spaces
a crowd of ways of losing grip

on its leaves because in it
a woman is eating its leaves,
her coarse breathing.

always wearing dark glasses
and always muttering: mother of dogs.
inside, my gun's trained out.

Fatima used to play accordion while I worked
always wore dark glasses.
but she was biting holes in furniture

and dancing when it was my job to dance
finally she got a disfiguring tattoo:
flies around her lips

and wanting her gone I made a pact with the devil
in which I gave him not my soul, not my life, but her.
she left, banished.

she lives in that tree now
with her coarse breathing
and I've got to get her out

each recoil, cinematic, I try
by clapping my hands to crush the smoke.
and I worry about this pact.

problem is: you marry
anyone you murder and as the tree holds spaces
her eyes hold flickers

and she mutters every time I miss.

calling Rothenberg's dogs

clap clap my hands jackknife.
it'll be sunset and I'm never bringing
Rothenberg's damn dogs again

to run through all this golden corn—
can't tell their eyes from dots blown.

my animals, my cats
know the hieroglyphs
my claps make

in the sky's long blue trek
around these fields, and my whistle's
a tarpaulin crudely pulled together.

these dogs have walked a meditation
measuring nearly a hundred feet.

clap clap: a red hand ritual;
once I see a snout, a little windsock compressed

with bronze eyes like rotary snails at my tweaked whistle.
these dogs on a detached string I hope don't stray

as far as where those trees' black-green tips
spread ethereal delicacy

clap clap clap: burned red; I think my claps
just collect in a pond in the air.

wind shift the golden corn,

the afternoon's roughly put together
and the dogs are not finished with their thinking.

abject

another of my friends has died.
he may have died of hope

—the brighter the flame
the quicker the candle goes

to find out what his soul was like
I light a poem to him.

rip one
from a glossy little book

crumple it completely
touch the creases with a match.

watch a twisting viscous light
shake tiny ambers down

and climb, like a flower opens
flicker by flicker.

light bares:
that's the way you die

brace your feet:
your enemy is inscrutable.

this little immolation
ends with its mouth open.

expert at street drains

followed a sigh so far my eyes flickered,
chased by certainties I stumbled
into street drains, now make my way by
smell of mud, asparagus and wet tin

the ways smells sequence, you never
know how argument turns,
like miles of soured apple, eyes adjusted
to slow brown light and exploring's
like pulling apart thatch.

winds blow in carbonic, but if I extend
a hand out: screams. so when it rains
I sail a paper boat on the glass surface
in a dripping cistern or trace light membranes,
gutter bits, become part of the turns

and watch at shoe level the churning sidewalk crowds
capillaries of light in water, the turns,
we're all eels, swimming in a barrel.
learn where to wade and where to stand,
how to come out anywhere.

summer drains are dry and open.
dusk's gold tints concrete, the same
as those far churning flags,
and just feet from the feet of that park bench
I breathe from my grate,

watch buildings rise and smash into the setting sun.
wind, and the tiny smell of bursting stars.

get these paintings through the fence

holding these paintings up
to restaurant windows: what do
people do when confronted with such greatness?

I'm: exclamatory man. keep the shoulders
churning. the pose the smile while practicing
the gesture like the saint's pale left hand

according to these paintings life's full
of horses, cannon, of returning generals on dark background
martyrs, piercing sun though crushing storms,

angels with chaotic musclature, triumphant legions
and I've had to haul these all around all afternoon
all avenues and set them up on sidewalks.

walk out in traffic with *Lucretia Raped*, and how are we
to carry on after such classics? "but everybody's seen that,"
they hiss. "she looks hungry."

listen I've dragged these gilded frames around,
propped *Christ Entombed* up on sidewalk coffee stands "but
his hair is fussy, pale," they some times group

and say "not quite readable-
"*Moses In The Bullrushes*—or is that little Botticelli—
what is he <u>smiling</u> at?" to turn *Saint And Executioner* around.

Picasso eyes two separate
insanities they fuss "decoration as a metaphor"
-"no, decoration as the whole thing,"

I splay my fingers out, and smile.
"the wrenched eye's the thing"—they snicker.
they walk by with their obvious little dogs

"observe the tug between subject and rendering."
"-installed two vanishing points."
Guernica. "-but nobody rides horses any more."
and nobody misses these. now I have them

propped up on cold park railing. observe behind
the railings asphalt pack of hungry dogs,
listen to the crashing bottles. wire and stars above
and people walking around calling people in the dark.

just up to me to show these paintings round.
drag them through each evening fence.
the night's rectilineal, fathomed and beyond, rain clouds gather
and a little sulfurous light crutches through the evening trees.

abyss

for throwing fists on the school bus
the gray and toothed country driver
drives me two miles further
into the torn farmland before letting me off
and I climb down followed by a shower of books
and spit filled soda cups, scuff the dirt
and turn in a chipping wind to walk all the way back
over a slack country road
which a distant yellow sunlight ruins
falling there and there on briar.
I kick my bag so many times it spews
and the wind catches
and then I'm chasing my things
into the reaching trees' scraped color
but suddenly the whole floor fails
as if the ground is snatched from the afternoon,
the land's deranged. drops, twists and plunges
and I stop my fall
clinging to bastard roots
into a vacuum I'd never seen.
below, a crawling abyss.
a dark, blurred, rough, sound filled subtraction
as if an evacuated ocean
had abandoned trees and rocks in crackling descent

the granite pulling sunlight down
on its breaking cold tints

an uttering void.
at bottom the noises of origin.
a metallic river shunts
and labors in its earthbound clumsiness
brute hinged and glistening between vising banks
and I'm in the blind roots of a breathing tree
my muscles looted by the chasm
my scalp frozen. my nausea pirouettes.
I watch birds so far they look like pollen,
inchlight fills the valley.

vacancy maps

it started in the humid weeks. people tired and tieless at public park
recitals and the hot underside of evenings were pushed along
like water sodden barges by rows of people's oscillating hand held
    fans.
I stood shabbily in back of crowds.

one evening there was a scuffle, the performance stumbled, never
was the same. the following day's newsprint reported a man
seen deftly disappearing during the C-major fugue,
lights on revealed conductor's score missing

and the papers snide: opportunity was always there,
they said, and hinted at planned high level heist.
soon after, other city things went missing: patches
of grass outside the courthouse. fingers from statues.

once from my window I saw a woman
on a rooftop wearing only shoes; everyday something
gone. due to phone line cross-ups I started getting
hissing phone calls. no names.—and I'm an utter nobody

but the urgency on the wires—I begin
to feel important now involved in some arcane
drama. so I start to strut and you know how little, bitten
people won't let that go.

well anything can be found—in taxis, pawnshops—
but first it must be declared missing. later discovered,

great relief, best if police with slow eyes interviewed
slow speech, reveal several missing, few found. more things now.

investigations, informants; stings are set. newspapers
howl about the growing problem, and my first real appearance:
a tiny face in crowd around official excavation
where one's dredged up. another on a truck at dock

certificate of authenticity intact. more sour
detectives hired, transferred, rehired. they open local offices
where you go in, peruse photos lining gray walls
and there I am, at lost-and-found, still looking

a bit pale, rudderless and knocked about. but on the street
I'm walking straight. when the police start handing out
vacancy maps I'm there, I'm snapped, profile,
staring at their biggest exhibit, a field of footprints.

and now my photo's on p. 27 of the paper. small, of course.
but the next sting pulls in a college professor, dentists
a priest, a cello player—everybody's in—I sip
my coffee, scan the news and try a quiet smile

the face always wins. waiting, I get phone calls coming in.
nameless criminals seeking plea bargains so they can get back on
    the street.
well, a bit of insolence lays the whole city before you:
I grant bargains. call the newspapers. announce more things missing.

one night, suddenly two rough interviews with police, rooftop.
I'm cleared. then I'm included in a press release. learned some
enigmatic phrases and look, here, now, today, I'm actually up to
news page 3—a small portrait, in savory grays of course,

me. gazing at the horizon. my eyes are focused, clear
and steady. like I'm in the know.

possession

she takes possession with her laugh
its confidence delicate as jasmine
it takes the room
its dainty to and fro

she has one elbow on the kitchen zinc,
feet languorously crossed.
here it is
like water closing in ringlets,
a delicate putting together.

whisper

I've let my telephone ring
hello? remembering
like searching in dirty water
by flashlight
that voice: hello. hello?
come on, I whisper.
shadows, like fish move.
play the tape again
for ripples. hello? kitten
under a car. a click
it always ends
the way a small twig breaks.
each replay is like running my finger
round a fine stemmed glass.
if I had my fingers on her throat
I would know who it was.

shift shoe

across city windows dusk's like
shattered bottles. there's only love.
not even that. in my
apartment, to the corner of the wall
I've pinned up a sheet, pulled up
a potted palm. and she and I
are dancing

shift shoe, turns and in
these empty rooms we breathe
our periodic tread
our blind advances, her red lips,
our shuffle, my dark hair gleaming
my radio's tinny flouirishes
and the rustle of her dress.

tango

evening's a painterly amber
returned from decorated sleep
the heat glistens, sweet and murky.
crickets radiate from trees.

my bare wood floor; a ceiling fan
slight red wind over hills outside
the window and now she puts a tango on.
a piano fills with chords

her look unrolls. she puts
my hand on silken hip. her eyes
savage territory
but each turn's spread butter

her black hair, curve
her look's black nets
thrown across reflections. her ears
platinum, her mouth half open

black heels across the flatness of my floor
each turn is a vessel, a glove
pulled gracefully inside out
a soft new light and the setting of the stars.

the day's later light

the day's later light, inward crowded, moves
umberish through densely scumbled brush
and bears come, no central axis in their lunges
just basal shifts, mythical and moody

bears: their whole lower vocabulary smells of soot;
scavenging on their rough ankles, the ones I have in mind,
through empty trees in grained-quartz winter light,
clustering, with shoved breath, they're black clogs

with coarse faces that pitch and yaw;
they tear at wet and pulsing things.
the weather shifts from light to black a thousand times with wind
in trees; them ambling as inward
as marbles rolling in dim bowls these bears pass,
the woods quiet as dank water in the bottom of still jars.

Nebraska, walking

there's one overhead black wire that runs to the horizon.
the sky walks its lightnings. the weather's
a glorious shorthand, an inhabited idea of unnumberable rhythms,
wind, three curves at a time and thunder
shudders like hollow trestles overhead,
and out of each next canyon
come clouds like squids crawling out of shoes.
wind howls iridescent. the scut and scut
of these blown plains. the one black wire we follow sways
to distant point past a broken trailer; a rural phone booth.

after the storm it looks like spray lifting from a sea
and an eerie copper glow, and after the clouds pass
there's a colossal light. birds pluck the wire
and adjust their intervals with terrifying little fights.
we walk in wet overcoats and boots, shuffle over dislocated feet,
watch as the corners of the nebraska sky ignite.

magnets in my boots

I walk a tilted, rifled walk
among tin cans, wing nuts,
my ankles tangled in ribbon steel
and on, pieces clustered to my feet.
I walk unshirted, glistening

the sky's a thousand empty spaces. the whole night's
a bridge made rickety by my walking
I'm trailing pins, wire snippets, bottle tops
bicycle spokes,
cotters, washers glitter

breathe and think this clear sky;
your gaze is the inside of this northward search.

secrecy

my son, who's brought his concertina, is standing in the middle of
    KS knee-high in grain which concertinas in waves of light
broken stalks of sun in martial drifts
in a vast field exhausted of its own waves
a hat over his pot-shaped haircut.

but the interior, the soul of KS is like that:
ever waves of light, making the ground move under my son's feet
—KS is like that, sky over endless wheatlands—
if you take a picture anywhere it looks like a sash window
top frame sky over bottom wheat, which you can pull
the sky down and the field up

the whole scene gloriously free
of the folding and bending marks you find in Yonkers or Peru
    where
clouds just rotted out collections of grumbles.

my son is a small man with a full beard
his clothes and hat are Bible-cover black
and he has never had his intentions bent
and he trusts KS
USA trusts its midland wheatlands wearing them
casually like a sash

my son has humped shoulders like a little formal buffalo
slow scooping eyes behind wire glasses around which the skin,
made white by sun, hardly moves

my son grows gossamer wings of thought
which he's not aware of, unbalanced bifurcating awkward wings
and he looks everywhere below the line of shifting grass
searching for whatever: rollerskate parts, peels of orange, blown-in
parrot shrieks from Uruguay
but her searches diligently, trailing his concertina
a small smile shaped just inside his beard

while the rolling light makes his feet meander
and all the wheat stands up like static bristle—
all the shifting grass up for the light grains
up for the circulation of independent air blown over all the stalks
which aggregation of dryness
doesn't touch my son's hint of wings which glint

and gently I have to tell him what he's found
not fact. but bridge to fact: that KS is flooded with brilliant but
    rolling light.

his small smile. eyes little paper loops of approval
and he wants to hold my hand, to concatenate a human link
against all that wind. like that to go on, son and father
linked in a W, bringing his concertina I suppose
breathless searching all that amber grain.

sahara eye

I asked her to help me move this plate glass across the desert
because dusty though she had ivory recoils
and both our hands folded around the upright edge
we began dryly pushing across the bleached gravel
as the sun made resonant lathed whistles

heat sneezes in all directions
the bottom edge scraped and
sand bits pin and tingle against the glass

refracted light on the grit, floating lilies in dry strings
palms acrid

crickle and scrape, dry bushes to your hopes
brown earth on her lips
and crisp sand

our breath as if hot-ironed
parched, we forgot
in broken shoes and pin sounds
getting the plate glass over the next dune
end on end the glass was a narrow slit

the sky so clear a white bird was an alien piece of paper.

several days; and I know she was losing faith
by the crisp turns of mascara in her look, sniff of turned head
and the movement of her dress revealing coffee shadows

but at night
the tingle of warm grit

thinking, if the desert is the answer to our mud-baked prayers
and burned buildings across hardened hills
looking from afar like death with missing teeth

in the distance there was only movable dust for wind.

when she became exhausted she turned
a pose of abandonment, her hand pulling up one foot
brutally exposing the crotch

we pulled and dragged
dry, our conversation needed fillet and tightener, then came
the hoarse cough of a storm
corrugated light
and grand hisses of water
wet pebbles sneezed in all directions.

when the rain cleared
sniffs, puddles and ochers
squeezed mud ribbons
and sinking fingertips of water

a piece of bent metal in a puddle.

start again;
the crackle of glass-edge
on washed split pebble.

a lull in the fighting

mauve smoke drifts off the brown hills
and trees still with crackling echoes
and here a few men sleep on the ground with rifles,
blood on the sleeve under dust scattered leaves

they are a cluster of facial abandonments
and streaked and twitching necks.
they surrender their dreams to dusk collective
the woman with amber breasts

and this side of the hills evening comes
glint by glint, a slow heavy alignment. dusk's arrival
always a lowering. she lifts her skirts and sits.
far droves of cattle drift

and the last sun leaves a rind on the tips of hills
and she begins a dream midsentence with wood incense,
with a smoked whispering,
she begins the way a bird lands.

the words with foreign hesitations, sibilances and cadence
a mouthing, eyelids plumskin,
as woodgrain swirls around knots, these soldiers' dream
exhales, and slows the air, inhales exhaustion

and she talks and gradually adjusts her hips.
beyond, clouds move by inward creasing,

trees begin to paint a breeze on the dusk.
a point of noise collects in this. it travels the length of the hills

and one soldier's awake by stitch, a muffled sneeze,
to find the evening has turned. the men are afoot
with curses. their rifles collect muttering
the dream ends. broken off

and a splintering fear from edge to point,
raise the rifle tips and search flitting from grass
stalk to twig to grass. their eyes collect
on some trees which are eating air on the edge of a storm.

folded roofs

this city's folds and streets, cement
and darkly rusted tin and buildings' doorless
entryways; it's a growth of rooms and slowly
shifts the light each day

I have a pair of artificial wings. dappled
rustling, richly feathered and with distant tips
I leave my door open
to climb up stairs of floors and floors

of dusted windows; stand upon the building's roof
where wind swerves the gravel. the same wind
that stiffens buildings scatters in their white distance
the mountains like bright whole cloth sent fluttering by fans

and my hair creases slowly in the wind.
I'm lean. my arms are strong my gaze straight
if slightly melancholic.
pointing north my wing tips

below them, day's leavings. evening's
exhausted, guttering and the streets like drained boats
in a floating monochrome of radios' songs;
dusk's a fugue among arches where the air is still.

wind catches these feathers' edges, wind pulls
the wings' lengths. At the edges of the city

are congratulatory little lifts: spires, poplars
and in the lowering sun the view's almost like water

strewn with rooftops, some flat,
some folded; these wings beat slow.
the whole horizon's come detached.
evening's a water-rush gatherer, floating.

factory girl

night hours all of this is dark blots
under the rustle of dry skies. but it's noon
and this is Phoenix. we're surrounded

by sepia, bistre, nineteen shades of ocher,
brown and hot iron scaffolding and in the air hangs calcite wash

which adds a satiny blur.
my car's glass glints watery
and my factory girl grins and laughs

I roll up the windows, I know
I can have any kind of sex I want and the only time
the window's down again is when she throws

another beer bottle out; a factory girl, rough
glint eyed and raucous but she has good foundry techniques.
noon's dust; the cricket's anesthetic;
gold dots crown the sun and in our lush rising
    sparks she harvests brilliance.

drawing

my face is no part of this. drawing,
I plan to make a morning
with my gray brush first filling
in windows, the underside of shoes,

coins on a table. next brush
for the foligage green. silver white
for snail glister and fog cut
from the mountainside and floating windskins

but kids, painting, don't plan.
you can't pare beige off pebbles
and a child first fills paper
with paint and lines

next walks around it. looks for things.
—is it a house?—a horse? the sigh
of February worms through
the blind and pressing soil?

glint by glint the making collects
in the child's face. in the kid's morning
the breeze makes billows of birds eyes,
and a canyoned stream looked into the making
   through its tumbled lenses.

storm

in the weather's electrified
winter twitches these two sisters spring
on the beach, a barefoot dance
to the drum of the storm
and they plan with their feet

what to do with a man.
as their heels skip
so shall his heart. flicker
the ghost of their shadow on sand
so dance on his pale soul

and this fling
their craft under these
slaughtered clouds muddled
with voltages
so squall his breath

cut his thoughts, and in
the misgathered edges of ocean
which tears from its floor
evict sleep and give him no peace.

squint

tips of branches scrape my glass
and I wake into a splintering
there's a bird thrusting in the twigs.
cocky bastard. lips stretched back
eyes squint. its song rips the air
so sharp you can feel behind.
the soil below its tree is cold and still: tidal.

damn bird again. its song's intricacies inhale
and waking's as if, along roof edges,
putting in a shoelace by feel.
begin again. as if tapping on a soupcan
to get all sleep out. bird's finger
in my face. day shifts incremental.
bird's now sitting on a vibrating sun.

by night

by night my voice gets deeper
fingers the ocean bottom,
craves your skin.

beach days have your eyes;
hovering in the wind's satin whorls
and rivulets, the way air currents turn.

by dusk your eyes and my voice
move together; we are the evening ocean
slow, water and air, ambulating in the late sun.

day of Esther's cat

but in matters of justice this century advances
slow as a gang of pick wielding laborers.
just a shuffle of everything common

even the day of the year commemorating, with a small
pilgrimage for justice, the day of Esther's cat in which
this walking band, that first played

in 1912, originally had a bearded man with eyes
the color of old photographs, and just as now
two dry violins, a clarinet, a stained trombone

and all process, in broken light
past the town's wintry cattails, trees and clouds
always followed by another man also in a long coat

reverently carrying a piano's innards
—relic of another year, another beating.
past the sagging village latchgates

past windows misaligned and each year
the procession path is tightly lined by the same
hissing teachers, wagoners, dour police

tattered girls, rachitic beggars, all
cursing, and suspicious women, doubt
in all their curved shoulders.

a couple of children follow carrying amulets
and lamps. all wind past the little
gardens raw and stirred

with the idiot Esther following.
the mayor walks in front, collector
of difficult questions. as they tread

clays softly burst from ground. the music's
worn and sinks and swerves in disrepair
and the bands wends slowly past

these contemptuous tobacco-chewing spitwits
and police who snarl and shove, trying
to disperse them with shouts out

how this is all monstrously allegorized.
all the instrument players' eyes down
they tread stony fields, they come now

trudging to the river. down to the same spot
where, once, when sadistic Bruno had tried
to drown his cat, Esther had

splashed into the water, saved the cat,
pushed Bruno under. now Esther stands
in the slipping river, holds up her arms

and grins her idiot grin. each year
she almost lets the water rise
and touch her crotch

—almost. the walking band lets Esther frolic
the rest of the procession, pulling her skirts up:
—jealous looks from roadside women.

and all weave toward the skyline which seems,
in winter, like sticks in viscous medium
and slow with birds stretched like rags across the orange sun.

and a scattering of applause
for this breakthrough: for overcoming
the anxiety of influence. and distantly they wend

to the horizon, the music eventually cut by tree trunks
and tin lamps disappearing one by one.
a few more years of this, and the century will be
patted into place. just a shuffle of everything common.

orchard dogs

summer's end, the orchard's flickering to a stop
trees begin the stiffness of their thoughts.
a ragged stillness. trees like statues flung
round with damaged arms against the congealing mist.
now the sky's coloring like pulled grease; and rains; and lightning
with its lobster's gait through clouds; thunder brings dogs,
dogs like noise and delight in the disorder of its sequences.
dogs dot the orchard. they scratch and bark to make a space,
tails bent up, the ground needs tearing at:
underneath the soil's delirious with roots.
dogs barking through this awkward pause,
its ordinary moments, to let erupt the opening of tips.
eventually apples emerge
as bubbles click to the surface of murky water.

waiting on a chair

either side, from this wood chair
this empty corridor, segue of dim focuses:

I sit outside my uncle's cheap and empty room,
with cigars. a tin basin should he need it
water and a sponge—

—this whole hotel is hung with air: something clings.
inside the door he's fighting with his prostitute again

my uncle's bald. she's an old doll, hollow
mascara-eyed. they're under the sheets.
she spits and through the door I hear her slaps

and clawing. groans when he tries to take her
spinal curses, noises muffled and adrift
seep through the corridor

I sit patiently outside his door
with comb and mirror should he need it.
shift my wooden chair.

eventually, outside the windows
evening comes, dismantling and delicate
and when my uncle cracks the door he's bruised and limping

boy—he softly gruffs—light my cigar. I sponge his face
the lip is cut, one wincing eye, his hair awry
the rest just slovenly indifference

and though the doorcrack's thin most evening
I try to see her. all I glimpse: a bare leg, her cigarette
—or its her eyes flare and extinction

and no complaints: she turns away with delicate cough.
boy—here—I slick his eyebrows. rub
brilliantine in his moustache to make it glisten.

then he slams the door again. all I hear's
uprooted breath, receding comments
to give her little gifts and presents.

it'll be quiet in this corridor tonight
if I want music I'll have to softly whistle.
this wood chair. I'll grope for matches later
peer either side as all these walls are feathered in anemic light.

my couch wants to be water

my room, mistaking its inside for night,
the light collecting under lamps. we
were ungrounded, afloat on the tide on the turn
with the pales of her full dress in lifts
and falls and as if rowing; her eyes lifted,
her attention finally to the scattering of oar dips,

her murmuring, the odor of pulled nets
dragged sand and rivulets, she's everywhere
in drifts and warbles and we're the folded
sides of river banks trying to rhyme in
tightening and loosening but misfitting,
her elongation of the wrists, having to pull

apart, to try again; alignment, augmentation,
river edges as two wet wrestlers; listen with my
sinews: cricket sounds as little mismatched springs,
mismatched wavelets here, eyes even
the new moon an erotic misfitting axel. she says

lets turn out the light on this
racket of brain and birds. let the dark
wind force open the branches.

night fight

this night's gloom is densely populated
with drunks, with cripples, thugs and tarts.
you hunt for faces, but no more do any
girlfriends come to your fights; it's the same
crepuscular abyss with eyes, and when
they turn the spotlight on
there's raw sweat on the ropes.

this is how the forgotten fight on.
a bell. the galleries fall quiet
and they let out the hooded thing
from the other corner; a scarred tonnage
with eyes like loose rings,
neck a democracy of knots.
the bell. headless yells drag
you both around the canvas
and you exchange blows to shake the lights.
fists to the mouth. fists to the eyes
echoes seem to copulate.
bell. he bleeds and the crowd's becoming
murderous. but you take an exit hit
misplaced; you, tattered, hop step
and find: this hall's the bottom
of some black painted thing, a cistern.
bell. begin the metered lurches of this fight.
a right. a cross. your ears die

and now you work in silence.
bell. sometimes in exhaustion
you and he weave together like a candle flame
fumbling in the dark. time to think
how once you scattered your hero's teeth.

bell. now rounds have sea waves'
impossible heaviness. somehow you're up
somehow he's up. somehow he's back
somehow the lethal punches come now
like a city bus pulling in at every stop.
now you're scrawling with your eyes closed.

the knockout.
like a pistol shot. comes first a mysterious
powdery light. crystallize the fight's heart:
now a silence. a dusk as if all drawn together by a knot

and a journey begins
to find—you're not sure what
but under this hall the soil is dark;
a blackness; perhaps like ink
spreads in uninhabited water.

body must find soul. it's quite
like looking for a long dropped, small coin.
you must, or you'll be lost on the return.
the face that was nowhere in the crowd.
and your movements as if carved from wax.

here it is. almost bent.
you and it fumble together. far somewhere
there's a scratch of noise
a candle tip that moves again.

the fight's medic pulls you out. oxygen.
in the audience people leave
as leeches crawl off something.

for three days you lie on a sodden
mattress under a shower head,
water quenching flame
it's a greenish cement room
and a floor hole you roll to

you pass blood. and in three days
you get your hearing back.
and notice the metallic dullness
of the window frame;

on the fourth day you drink
water from the iron sink.

Passiod's song

tennis balls sequentially under the trees.
plum-blossom lips, she sits languid
in waves of dappled sun, a beauty
in the afternoon. men walk and talk in bronzed
percussion. her hat's white and curved:
a beauty with a sloping neck,
her laugh a spill of paper cups

and I'm so good at insolence. my blond
curls composed, all the glossies show
my eyes wet as lynx's. gaze, gaze:
I wear such narrow fawn colored shoes

and I like betraying married women.
I'm a gigolo who cruises garden parties,
tea rooms—how your distaste
expands me. I'm silken
in my form-fitting jacket;
I say things, she'll overhear, weave
a filament of hopelessness through my voice,
smile, turn to find a waiter, turn back
and—look, she's taken off her ring.

my smile's cream-colored silk,
my voice well done and well buttered.
you want to warn her—you think?

rubies slither. I am their facets,
intricate and scuttling,

and you—but the sun just wanders in your scaffolding.
she thinks too. she's, she believes, mistreated;
sensitive, but mirror proud; now as rewards
for past pain she'll let herself
be worshipped

I have nocturnal breath, my smiles,
and deftly beveled insolence; you want
to tell her now?—
the clock ticks as a spiderwalk.
she pulls her gaze away and it comes back
like brought dishes with covers.

gaze upon my tailored cuffs, my decorated
socks. inhale my curled perfume: of course we talk.
the evening sky has golden joints.
and yes of course we mate. one time
she's an ecstasy in blown glass with end
twisted off; another time her mouth
gaped open to emit the strike of bronzed bells
but they remain up and frozen; one time

my walls wash in and we are creaking ships
in bursting seas, the crack and flay
of salt and wind, her breaths
like rabid fish through waves, she comes
down trembling and slowly
as a boat propelled by bent machinery
prow rises, mouth rent
her ship raises, water sparks
and lowers again in the wrong cuts

I have glossy photographs to show all that
which I've sent now to her husband.
gaze upon my garnet-red links, their facets
and on my curls again.

but she and I will meet once more. a foggy dawn
at a coffee shop just opening
and you can hear the cooks, and banter
cross hand remarks and thrown cans
the smell of oils and bread cooking.

he'll have beaten her.
her eyes as floor mess swept up,
her voice's paper boats
spread across a pond and wobbling;
she wears her hat brim down

well, gaze and gaze: the horizon's provided
for you, a horizontal line—
how I expand in your disdain. my elegant
fingers, satin sleeves, my handkerchief's a powder blue;
gaze upon my oyster-liqueur eyes;
you're entangled by my gestures.
gaze upon my petal-soft necktie.
envy my narrow hips.

cello

malign and moan, cello's bi-pupilled eye
cello's breath grunting and caught
lopes over passages of bare earth

first notes like gray sheep
in unselective groupings, barely legible.
cello's dragged breath, adjusted. draws
wet birds to flight, measured
from the point of departure.

you can move again avoiding
abscessed walls and predatory lights
but always in this hotel the night begins
meticulously quiet in quiet hallways

then cello recalling first promises,
cello sumptuous, Italinate, figurative
apertured, translucent and high strung

all evening, falls to writhes and daubs
its little fricatives, garroted breaths
always in the next room

the dividing corset.
this is what happens between fathers and daughters
cello's stuck open, breathing

and on, the way it moves, this is
what happens between brothel habitués and dancers

as silk moves under silk by transom light
cello's elegant as secrecy
and in the darkness of interior.

so sling your arm with confidence around a cellist,
feel the bow as caliper lowering
on melancholy horizontal fields,
lowering on a sunset.

light and assemble candle lights: the bow
moves slowest in a moving horizon;
her clothes: the bow's
a slow blade that's cut lilies into deranged white,

and metering the cello's breath
place your fingertip along the strings
feel the cello's wood grain shudder, mauled
and the cellist vibrate.

lessons from a cat on waiting

light fades like soiled feathers blown around by fans.
my cat waits well, drapes herself
over my head and her eyes of spun bronze
spread oars across another of her tangent silences:
half lidded she arranges waiting
into larger and larger rooms, and I begin to sleep.

and I awake again in gloom to the sounds of billiards clicking.
tiny angel rejects are floating down again
if they have hair, it's lovely mustard yellow
many of them don't—instead, red grease-pencil
cancellations across their brows and heads:
with skewed lace wings they come

scattered, dropped from some eternal factory.
each may have expected corinthian notes
with its descent but each, with one foot
twisted or fingerless or with dislocated eyes
that struggle with the air around them

and swept from the billowing stars
falls to sidewalk where cat eats it.
as it hops along the ground with miscast platinum voice
and tiny nostrils. it's not billiards clicking
but the snap of greasy little iridescent ribs.

and cat's back. sitting puffed beyond
real density with little curled back lips
and soft breath which starts here and ends here
waiting as thoughtful as fluid rolls around
in too big containers. cat's as black as space

her look, low slung, rhomboid,
almost sleeping with a pilot light on;
languid she turns her face to me and purrs,
in her eyes a distant lacewing dancing.

slow rented rooms

with smoke, night repeats as blackened pistons.
you wake to rust and leaking pipes
squirming on the ceiling, naked bulbs and an
outside squeal of brass. another day

loose scratched, indifferent, you might think
opening wet eyes that the heavens glisten in
fibrillating astronomical brilliance, but it's a dirty universe
vulgar little ceilings, odd sibilances

and all that banging on metal floors, unfitting copper.
you set your mind to innards of a camera gray, to pipes.
brackets. just a part among parts, and accessory to greasy walls

awake with the setting of the teeth into vacuity
and rise, to city wires, to wind in nickel apertures
and screwed aluminum plate. once more, scraped

breath. the hesitation. then through the rented door
once more; cap pulled down on dry hair
with a brief hiss.

a low sociopathic hotel

a low, sociopathic hotel with musty rooms for this reunion
I've already seen the drainwater, the cleaning maid
her mouth tumescent, composed when I saw her in the corridor
suddenly quiet, as a canary taken underground

this picnic's on the filmy grass with dandelions
and straw-hatted carousel-mouth salesmen,
the picnic's cook, somebody's nephew with a hockey stick
and two women, friends. the sky draws sly as mother-of pearl

and there's an apparition: a dirigible, softly overhead,
opalescent in its plump skin, aerated, feathering
its small propellers and almost like a bicep floating
in blue drawn glass—and not one
of those little sky exit-planes: it keeps drifting low, around.

the sky's almost rubbery in its iridescence, there's a low wind
carrying the odors of scratched verdigris out of neighboring wet
    woods,
and after meat and after wine my speech's as thick as mine dust

and carefully ignored by the cook with his wilting mushroom hat
and by Humphrey with the splits between his teeth,
I throw my leg over the first woman for her smile. I take
her breasts into my palms, she lifts her skirt

but the other woman, her close friend, insists she keeps
her coat cloaked near and keeps whispering advice. the sky's
    pastel,
the dirigible turns, silent, silvery, glistening and loose

and I can't concentrate. the dirigible's a piece
of silver perfection among torn clouds
and I keep thinking of the cleaning maid, that look.
I imagine I'll find things missing from my room;
I think of her tumescent pinks; I wonder how
I'll deal with her; that bold and tiny mouth.

at the Linnington Café

she called; we hadn't spoken for weeks. morning,
an outside table at the Linnington Café, in a shady ingathering
a nymph with white arms, alabaster teeth,

the waiter, a long elbowed heron, unblinking eyes.

a breeze shifted at her light skirts. we cast off and pulled
both at the oars,
now a small boat in wet seas, dipping and coming up
a glossy white wake, water spilling from the scuppers
and with a couple of jokes we passed buoys and bells,
waves, things to raise us

mention of rural economies,
worship of psychological gods

the wind stiffened and we set the sails, passing in the distance
the point of alienation
and the pursuit of ordinary life. this direction the prow rises.
I am magnetized by the rhythm of the troughs

a change in topics. the color of the waves now cobalt
and we tack

ropes and clinking, the clouds rough fluffy brutes on blue.

at the next table a couple puts down money and departs.
following them she has one eye for the street
      —there's Maggie

    —there's Henry
one eye for me.

a glance in the sky, watching the wind,
eack privately geometrizing our theories.
another drink? soda and alchemy.

we start again. proceed by worm gear.

a dip in the overhead light
and we turn by degrees, pulling again, and she's a bit ardent,
next zealous. now of territoriality. loss of speech in the orang-
  outang.
she opposed to the principles on which old society is based.

dipping, cresting, we turn in, rowing again. we look
for points of light on the shore; the wandering of the waterline.

and to the shallows, where everything softens to cabbage water and
  clay,
the wavelets here are brittle and seldom.

she takes a breath; the parting of the palm fronds. her glance.

she wants money.

a veil, her eyes are following the shallows;
a yawn, all the phases of the moon.

the twittering of birds flying up some far estuary.

I bicycled the desert

all across that bald horizon I had come
my wheel tracks sinusoidal, desert wind
in spokes make limp and untied vowels
and desert's breathing's a grid
of tiny dots bright and balanced
in wind dust and it was the sun's reflections on wire spokes

kept my bicycle up.
there, we married
under semi-transparent rice.
she too keeps the blue from swerving:
she threw my bicycle in a shed,
and breathes her hawk's wind high above.

the groin and grain of frosted land

the groin and grain of frosted land
its hacksaw dirges, its musculature; compressed horizons
and earth sunken from exhaustion; these
outlines look attacked by dogs; trees
in the pond of the sky, strainers for the empty winds

and night is the lift of a metal bowl, rolling
the sky upwardly, leaving trees as wake,
leaving stones in the ground, tilted hedgerows
and a wash of stars wrestling to find patterns.

in heat

in heat
this rooms's narratives are inclined to brutality—
are smudges of dirty blue. the wallpaper's savage choice
of colors orange, pink; their stem designs;
her naked thigh, the yellow pillow
the squirming red couch—and her suspicion
the incremental turning of the eye
the lizard's stare as twine—
                        where have you been
we talk.
outside, the sky's stylized smooth surfaces,
crickets braid, the mauve night
and her exaggerated hip, a slave to light
                        —and what is that

just people whispering under red trees
outside copper-green windowsills. and that—
the rustling of water in metal tanks
and we braid: love with suspicion,
with the night bird's song in improvised diagonals;

let sink in the sweet sound
    of succulent pink
        turns of petal
            after petal

savage breath—
primitive in the turn of the eye.

1930

a valley first starts collecting sounds, then odd scraps of color.
small arguments develop in the dark and kitchens coalesce:
a village grows in clustered yellows, piccolo pinks, red roofs
and there's the churning of disparate machines.
at first a cluster ragged and forgettable
but it becomes a town; with sky line

chewed; a cough, business arrives, another cough
to stop and start seeing again. it accumulates things around a core
of crumpled axioms, then urinals, air stuffed into crates, then trains
crystalline in cross whistles. the town's now sprawled
and half-flat, accumulates a freight yard's textural complexity
and a work force

becomes a town of people in little rented rooms
with the usual involuntary circles: heartbeats, breaths, orgasms
all under creosoted eaves which contain sighs, locked bedrooms,
    locked
closets. it accumulates holidays, when lines of yellow shades make
vertebrated streets and afternoons are stirred by fans.
and night life, taverns, with glistening piano keys, and dark streets
    smudged
with the small watercolors of prostitutes' dreams, growth again
and the treadle of fear under the table

growth again, plywood detonations and lobs of color
and on, and so on, mixture of mud and confectionary but salesmen
    fast

fast and assured and town acquires intersections gritty and
    embattled
and stiff-haired power poles and it grows rich and tuberous,
grows slate and iron, grows the stuff of industry.

after each day's soots clear,
night settles and the stars come out, masticated and glistening
in a wildebeest's teeth. there's stealth in this stretch of hills
and high aspirations. everybody knows the look:
cities are the bristling brightness of glass.

tin by tin

originally perhaps broken by sin
or by handmade horror

each of us in this hotel
has looked in mirrors with black spots
and seen our pupils as black spots

in rooms, wood by wood
linen by linen
evening breathes and a layering of dim lights

by night
to rehabilitate our relation with the cosmos
from chairbacks in a dim row
we all watch the universe.

tin by tin.
the bottoms of casement windows broken
people sit in lines, cello heads and taut necks

iron by iron, boards and neon
and under the satin, long breathing skies
compare the stars to whistling benzene

or make the night
a pond filled with dark water.

sitting in rows of folded fingernails
never saying what we see

the universe: its hand inclined in doubt.

978-0-595-38454-9
0-595-38454-4